POETRY FOR A MIDSUMMER'S NIGHT

Poetry for
A MIDSUMMER'S NIGHT

In the Spirit of
William Shakespeare's
A MIDSUMMER NIGHT'S DREAM

Marvin Bell

Paintings by
Mary Powell

O hell! to choose love
by another's eyes.

Seventy Fourth Street Productions
Seattle, Washington

Books by Seventy Fourth Street Productions
are available directly from the Publisher:

Seventy Fourth Street Productions

350 North 74th Street
Seattle, Washington 98103
206-781-1447 PHONE / FAX

"Being in Love" is reprinted by permission
of the author from *New and Selected Poems*
by Marvin Bell, Atheneum, 1987.
"White Clover," "Trees as Standing for Something,"
"To Dorothy," and "An Elm We Lost"
are reprinted by permission of the author from
A Marvin Bell Reader: Selected Poetry and Prose,
Middlebury College Press/
University Press of New England, 1994.

Ms. Powell's original paintings for this volume,
a series of midsummer night skies,
were done in oil on canvas, 12" x 24", 1997.

Publisher's Cataloging-in-Publication Data

Bell, Marvin,
Poetry for a midsummer's night : in the spirit of William
Shakespeare's A midsummer night's dream / Marvin Bell ;
oil paintings by Mary Powell.--1st ed.
p. cm.
ISBN 0-9655702-1-5

1. Shakespeare, William, 1564-1616. A midsummer night's dream--
Characters--Poetry. I. Powell, Mary Ruth. II. Title.

PS3552.E52P64 1998   811'.54
                                      QBI97-41377

ISBN 0-9655702-1-5

FIRST EDITION
───────────
02 01 00 99 98   5 4 3 2 1

This book is dedicated
to Dorothy Bell
and to Albert Sampson.

Special thanks
to Lani Jacobsen
and Peter Kahle.

Contents

Program Notes

Each year on the Saturday nearest the summer solstice, a motley band of friends assembles at the home of Kyle Iddings and Alison Grable in the North Beach section of Seattle, Washington, to perform a scaled down version of Shakespeare's "A Midsummer Night's Dream."

The house is built on a hill which affords three tiers of balconies overlooking a fire pit in a sunken backyard. Roles are handed out anew for each scene. There are spotlights and a sound system. A few corny props, costumes and masks complete the production. A sword, a helmet, the head of an ass....

The action begins after dark, with the audience shrinking and swelling as its members are called uphill to perform. Naturally, there is clowning and ridicule to go with food and drink and music. Those in the know bring light chairs and heavy coats. Lines are blown. Double entendres proliferate. The few who are theatre professionals — and there are some among us — labor to be amateurs. For the rest of us, being amateurish is duck soup.

Of course, staging the entire play is beyond us. The year we tried to do it all, we had progressed as far as what I regarded as my Big Scene when the police arrived. The neighbors had gone as long as they could. That led to a shortened version in succeeding years, and now the neighbors contribute umbrellas when needed and hang over the fence to watch.

The evening, like Shakespeare's play itself, is all about delight — in romance, in mystery, in puckishness and true love, in friendship, and preeminently in the language of poetry that twists and turns to follow our very insides.

Just as we savor a party in the spirit of Shakespeare's Romance, so we dream of a wide door for poetry readers. Shakespeare is not primarily for scholars and classrooms, but for making something of. On that Saturday night nearest the summer solstice, we make something of Shakespeare that is also ourselves.

Poetry is like that. Its effect occurs inside the reader ready for it. Inasmuch as Shakespeare's play gives us all the narrative we can handle, replete with adventure and spectacle, I thought to accompany it with a rational music. These poems are a kind of talk that might go on among those who know the play.

We do not take Shakespeare's place. We make a place for Shakespeare. That is, these poems are not the play, but are a play upon the play. I pray the reader will find them easy to enter and, through them, enter the theatre where the shades of Oberon and Titania, Hermia and Lysander, Demetrius and Helena, and of the trickster Puck glimmer in the recesses of our imagination as we relive the longest day, and quickest night, of the year.

M. B.

Cast of Characters

THESEUS, Duke of Athens

HIPPOLYTA, Queen of the Amazons, betrothed to Theseus

EGEUS, father of Hermia

LYSANDER, in love with Hermia

DEMETRIUS, in love with Hermia, favored by her father, Egeus

HERMIA, in love with Lysander

HELENA, in love with Demetrius

OBERON, King of the Fairies

TITANIA, Queen of the Fairies

PUCK, or ROBIN GOODFELLOW, a most mischievous sprite

PEASEBLOSSOM	*four*
COBWEB	*fairies*
MOTH	*attending*
MUSTARDSEED	*Titania*

PETER QUINCE, a carpenter	
NICK BOTTOM, a weaver	*as PYRAMUS*
FRANCIS FLUTE, a bellows-mender	*as THISBY*
TOM SNOUT, a tinker	*as WALL*
SNUG, a joiner	*as LION*
ROBIN STARVELING, a tailor	*as MOONSHINE*

Scene

The city of Athens and the Palace Wood nearby.

Of a Midsummer's Night

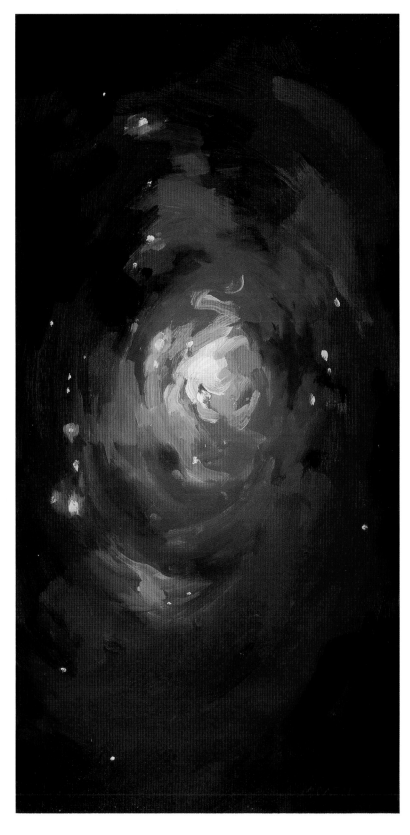

Hermia, Helena, and Will

Hermia, Helena, and Will

We begin with two young women.
Their hair twinkles among the trees.
Light that buffs the leaves leaves on them
the shine of chaste energy before
it drifts like dust to the forest floor.
In this celestial, angelic dust,
they play and take each other's truth
for granted. One must marry unhappily,
another not at all, if others have their way.
But something in the failing light
says Nature has a mind of its own.

They do not know a playwright holds them,
that by his hand their troubles lighten
until, like light itself, their troubles vanish.
How can it be? Is there such magic
in Nature, some brew that can reverse
a father, and the State too? It is unlikely,
and so they frolic, what else to do?
What is that dust that thickens
their eyes? Who has the power
to make right things go wrong and wrong
go right? Who is this Shakespeare?

On a midsummer night, the lovers dream
and are changed. They will act
in ways we can only imagine. They
are not themselves, but two who, like many,
find themselves ill-bethrothed
to love's best friend, or love's mere second,
and see their own best friend's heart
given to that very one they would resist.
Oh, it's a famous mess, you know the story.
The parents tell you whom to marry, but
it's your best friend loves him, not you.

Since all luck is dumb luck, they sleep.
The ladies sleep, and their dazed lovers
sleep, while fairy spirits wake
and seal with potions the lovers' eyes
until all can be made right, which is to say
each one loves right and is rightly loved.
Reader, read on and be assured:
our forest holds such fairy dust
as will in time turn four into two plus two.
For it is but a dream wherein love's lost
and love's puzzle left in pieces.

Love is in the dawning, not in sleepwalking,
in seeing that which is and is no other.
For if love be not love when love it seems to be,
then we are lost until such magic dust
can wake us to our senses.
So let midsummer's dreams hold sway
while dread tomorrow becomes beloved today.
Hail the Bard and those who tread the boards
and like to mix us up. We cannot make out
the women from the men who go about
in mask and costume, thinking we cannot tell
love's top from love's bottom, but we know it well.

Like Words, Like Music

Like Words, Like Music

Some have heard the music in the trees
that has no words, but words they have
more than music, and so they sing.

Others have heard the words of love
that make no sound, but sounds they have
more than silence, and so they speak.

For them, there's crackling music in a fire,
a round in the rapids, shimmery chords
midair, and a drumming in the earth.

What's worth more than our poverty
that needs such speech and song as poets
and lovers are helpless not to utter?

Lovers have a music in their heads,
the words by heart, and could not love long
were they less heartfelt, less headstrong.

Midsummer's a confluence of time
and passion, when those halfway to matrimony
labor to compose their love symphony.

Shakespeare knew his meters and strewed them
along the garden path and in the wood
that those who needed most to hear them could.

Lovers, though you be neither courtly nor English,
yet you have other traits worth a show,
so sing and play together, for you never know.

—

Demetrius to Hermia:

Being in Love

with someone who is not in love with
you, you understand my predicament.
Being in love with you, who are not
in love with me, you understand my dilemma.
Being in love with your being in love
with me, which you are not, you understand

the difficulty. Being in love with your
being, you can well imagine how hard it is.
Being in love with your being you,
no matter you are not your being being in
love with me, you can appreciate and pity
being in love with you. Being in love

with someone who is not in love, you know
all about being in love when being in love
is being in love with someone who is not
in love being with you, which is
being in love, which you know only too well,
Love, being in love with being in love.

At Wood's Edge

At Wood's Edge

Who passed this way cracked the fennel stalk.
There's anise in the air, and broom everywhere
and grass in bloom at wood's edge, so much of it.
The wild carrot has as good a mane as the lovers
who wandered here calling the Veronicas
to cease their purple posing and pity them —
young men and young women wishing to marry.

The earth has heard it all, for men stamp about
the forests every day, testing their patience,
and others, with an ear to the ground, moan
as if to hear there an onslaught of tenderness.
Nightly, the sun descends and the wind rises
until an otherworldly dark blankets the day
and holds the lovers, with what they cannot say.

Look at this one who thinks he's badly matched,
digging a hole, in which he throws his dreams,
while romance elsewhere opens her hands
as if to set her hopes free to fly at will.
This forest is all prickly pine and monkey puzzle,
all thorned holly bush, ruinous oak and ivy.
This path is for the lost, whose eyes grow heavy.

Or so they think, surrendering to sleep.
Best to cede this day to night and hope for better.
These are their days. They want something more.
They can hardly wait to see what's next in store.
They will fret as they must till everyone is mated.
But the lovers will grieve while the cast is feted
unless the stars bloom — and they're in no hurry.

At Night in the Forest

At Night in the Forest

Lion, wolf and bear contend, the owl clamors,
fairy and sprite dance to outdo Nature herself
whose love-tokens make a pulpy forest bed
on which beheaded roses bleed their last,
and weeds and worms devour as they must
that which lovers left to rot when it was not
the course of true love that they sought
nor long fidelity to nightly ins-and-outs,
the ups-and-downs, the catch-as-catch-can
that makes a marriage more than lovely
and bride and groom, woman and man.

What dove was that? Whose nightingale?
This place that offers neither straw nor grain,
but primrose sore with singing in the breeze,
makes the evergreen a bowstring frame
and cools the savage breast until it's tame.
Are we afraid, or only half-unmade
by crows and scent of carrion, by violets
drowsy and the hawthorns out of breath?
Who comes here from the night to be not seen,
appear, and teach us the tricks of your trade.
Put us to sleep and cause the dark to fade.

Puck's Mischief

Puck's Mischief

Puck's our fleet courier of dew, or such rubies
as light shining through water makes,
and floral crowns and such accessories
as blind a bat and mole but in the dawn
blow away, leaving blooms gone to seed,
a last wisp of steam where the jewels sat.

Robin Goodfellow! Some call you bad fellow,
whimsical spy, sprite of many faces,
aper of bear growl and wolf howl, misguider
of the lost, fond of the preposterous,
crazy like a fox, placer of briers and thorns
among the fronds that look right for a bower.

What flash of light where dark had free reign?
It's Puck, turning things upside down again.
What speech through stone walls, what bush talks?
Puck throws his voice and stops the clock.
Puck's the one ties knots in your dog's tail
and tricks us into thinking the real unreal.

Oiled by apricots and dewberries, by purple
grapes, green figs and mulberries,
Puck's tongue's never tied, nor his eye weary.
Philosopher of ends and means, he favors
alchemy and sorcery, potions and wit.
He does what he likes to, and savors it.

Oberon to Titania:

Five Oh's

Five oh's are but a single line of our life together.
Five ah's but a moment of our peace.
Five eureka's cannot contain what you have taught me.
Five aha's cannot express our expectations.
There are five ouch's for every oops!
And five oops's for every please.
And five please's for every don't.
And most of all, a dozen wills for every won't.

Love, you and I are more than one plus one.
Though we are two, two too is too few.
Love has defeated reason by all who tried.
No, we are like an hourglass upon its side.
It seems that one and one at times make three.
We overlap throughout Eternity.
A thousand oh's could not bespeak our wooing.
True love's surprised to know just what it's doing.

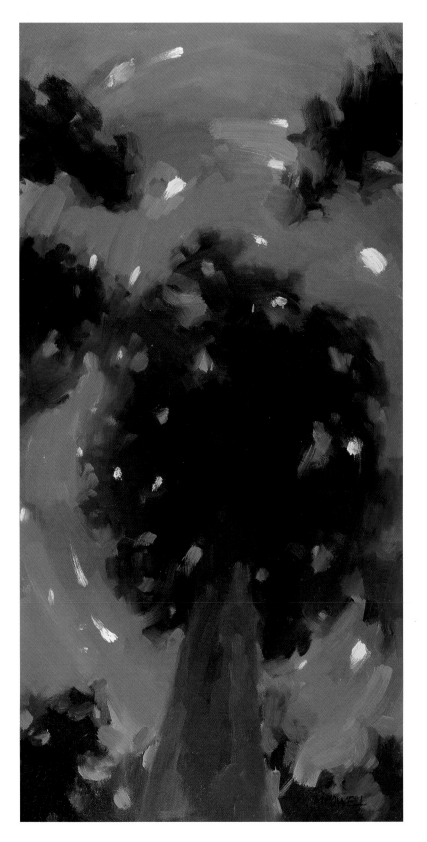

Trees Like Us

Trees Like Us

This tree that resembles a woman,
also resembles a man.

We were told not to make so much of nature
that it rivals a man and woman.

We were told but have heard
in the wind among the leaves

a breathing interrupted by a silence
in which the very air is suspended

for the time it takes a woman and a man
to stop time in its tracks

until the planet turns its face from the departing
light again, leaving behind a silence

in which the memory of a face
holds its breath until morning.

All night the trees whisper sweet nothings
that put us to sleep, then hold us.

Of Airy Nothing

Of Airy Nothing

"Knacks, trifles, nosegays, sweetmeats, messengers,"
bribes, favors, baubles, charms and trinkets,
lures, enticements, bait, a king's ransom.
Details, details — you'd think it meant their lives
the way the lovers carried on about
whom they saw or couldn't see or wouldn't see,
and who's a donkey and who's a donkey's backside.

The fact is, all of them were taken in
and for good reason, having none themselves
unless it's summer that's to blame,
what with bursting berries beside the lover's lane
and the ripest apple unable to wait, fallen.
Each year the lovers listen and the forest hears.
At wood's edge, the willow weeps new tears.

Now caution fails, good sense departs,
sensation collars those who might have married
otherwise by prearrangement, but warmed
by the musky dew that cushions late blooms,
now look for their heart's delight, receptive to
whoever first comes near or into view.
Above the forest canopy, the sky is blue.

By thistle, blossom, cobweb, moth and mustard,
by stalks and stems, by leaves the forest brews,
love chases love till nothing's left to lose.
The Muses hardly know which one to choose.
Reader, don't you love it when you know
who's who and what's what, especially who?
A play within the play, and then we're through.

In the last scene, the music nearly plays itself,
Nature blesses every nook and cranny,
and whoever was offended has Robin's word
that farce makes fools of all without intent.
By curtain call we all know what was meant
was less a wild goosechase in the woods
than a playful whiff of love's midsummer scent.

How the Lovers Found
True Love After All

They say the woods are full of mystery,
who venture in and do not reappear
until such time as they achieve a mastery
of signs employed by sprites, who feel no fear.

Not so, the lovers, who, not knowing better,
scatter their emotions like plucked daisies
across the forest floor, some sweet, some bitter:
spasmatic measures of how much love is crazy.

The trick's to have the one you love in view
when he or she can see no one but you.
It helps, to get the other in the mood,
to call them out at night to walk the wood.

People will tell you the forest has its way
with those who walk it all-worked-up.
Desperate, lonely, lovesick every day,
they sniff the devil's paintbrush, the buttercup.

Who can predict when Cupid's state is bliss,
and Eros can spare an amorous advance?
Our lovers, heretofore astray, amiss,
found true love's path by the seat of their pants.

POEMS FOR AFTER THE CURTAIN HAS COME DOWN

White Clover

Once when the moon was out about three-quarters
and the fireflies who are the stars
of backyards
were out about three-quarters
and about three-fourths of all the lights
in the neighborhood
were on because people can be at home,
I took a not so innocent walk
out among the lawns,
navigating by the light of lights,
and there there were many hundreds of moons
on the lawns
where before there was only polite grass.
These were moons on long stems,
their long stems giving their greenness
to the center of each flower
and the light giving its whiteness to the tops
of the petals. I could say
it was light from stars
touched the tops of flowers and no doubt
something heavenly reaches what grows outdoors
and the heads of men who go hatless,
but I like to think we have a world
right here, and a life
that isn't death. So I don't say it's better
to be right here. I say this is where
many hundreds of core-green moons
gigantic to my eye
rose because men and women had sown green grass,
and flowered to my eye in man-made light,
and to some would be as fire in the body
and to others a light in the mind
over all their property.

Trees as Standing for Something

Trees as Standing for Something

1

More and more it seems I am happy with trees
and the light touch of exhausted morning.
I wake happy with her soft breath on my neck.
I wake happy but I am happier yet.
For my loves are like the leaves in summer.
But oh!, when they fall, and I wake with a start,
will I feel the sting of betrayal and ask, What is this
love, if it has to end, even in death,
or if one might lose it even during a life?
Who will care for such a thing?
Better to cut it down where it stands.
Better to burn it, and to burn with it,
than to turn around to see one's favorite gone.

2

It began when they cut down the elm and I let them.
When the corkscrew willow withered and I said nothing.
Then when the soft maple began to blow apart,
when the apple tree succumbed to poison,
the pine to a matrix of bugs, the oak to age,
it was my own limbs that were torn off, or so it seemed,
and my love, which had lived through many storms,
died, again and again. Again and again, it perished.
What was I to say then but Oh, Oh, Oh, Oh, Oh!
Now you see a man at peace, happy and happier yet,
with her breath on the back of his neck in the morning,
and of course you assume it must always have been this way.
But what was I to say, then and now, but Oh! and Oh! Oh!

To Dorothy

You are not beautiful, exactly.
You are beautiful, inexactly.
You let a weed grow by the mulberry
and a mulberry grow by the house.
So close, in the personal quiet
of a windy night, it brushes the wall
and sweeps away the day till we sleep.

A child said it, and it seemed true:
"Things that are lost are all equal."
But it isn't true. If I lost you,
the air wouldn't move, nor the tree grow.
Someone would pull the weed, my flower.
The quiet wouldn't be yours. If I lost you,
I'd have to ask the grass to let me sleep.

An Elm We Lost

On it we wrote a little essay
about who loved who.
Shade moves in the grass, never still,
and they still do.

Photo: Kate Garfield

MARVIN BELL lives in Iowa City, Iowa, and Port Townsend, Washington. He is the author of fifteen books, including *The Book of the Dead Man, A Marvin Bell Reader, A Probable Volume of Dreams* (winner of the Lamont Award), *Stars Which See, Stars Which Do Not See* (a National Book Award finalist), and, with William Stafford, a book of poetry written as correspondence. He has received awards from the Academy of American Poets and the American Academy of Arts and Letters, and has held Guggenheim and NEA fellowships as well as Senior Fulbright Appointments to Yugoslavia and Australia. Mr. Bell has been a Woodrow Wilson Visiting Fellow, a Lila Wallace-Reader's Digest Writing Fellow, and a faculty member at Goddard College and the Universities of Hawaii, Washington, and Iowa. Currently, Mr. Bell is Flannery O'Connor Professor of Letters at the University of Iowa Writers' Workshop.

Photo: Jeffry Boyce

MARY POWELL lives on Bainbridge Island, Washington. She holds a BFA from the University of California-Berkeley, and has also studied at the Art Center College of Design, Los Angeles; the University of Guanajuato, Mexico, Art Institute; and with Ron Lucas, Seattle. Ms. Powell's illustrations appear in *Wildflowers of Sierra Nevada*. She has done illustrations for the Ministry of Education in Ethiopia, Africa, where she taught art and English for two years. A painting instructor and former gallery owner, Ms. Powell has had a number of shows, including Society of Western Artists, California; Harbor Gallery, Bainbridge; and in Seattle at the Frye Museum, Alexis Hotel, Seafirst Plaza Building, Jeffrey Moose Gallery, and Washington State Convention Center. She describes herself as an oil painter who paints "as directly as possible, the fewer fussy strokes the better, always searching for beautiful color relationships."

Other Books by Marvin Bell

Wednesday: Selected Poems 1966-1997 [1998]

Ardor (The Book of the Dead Man, Vol. 2) [1997]

The Book of the Dead Man (Vol. 1) [1994]

A Marvin Bell Reader: Selected Poetry and Prose [1994]

Iris of Creation [1990]

New and Selected Poems [1987]

Drawn by Stones, by Earth, by Things that Have Been in the Fire [1984]

Old Snow Just Melting: Essays and Interviews [1983]

Segues: A Correspondence in Poetry (with William Stafford) [1983]

These Green-Going-to-Yellow [1981]

Stars Which See, Stars Which Do Not See [1977]

Residue of Song [1974]

The Escape into You [1971]

A Probable Volume of Dreams [1969]

Things We Dreamt We Died For [1966]

POETRY FOR A MIDSUMMER'S NIGHT was set in Bembo,
a text type noted for classical beauty and readability.
Bembo is modeled on type cut by Francesco Griffo
in Venice, Italy, in 1495. It takes its name from its first use
in Aldus Manutius' printing of *De Aetna* by Pietro Bembo.
A standard typeface in Europe since its origin, Bembo was
redesigned for the Monotype Corporation in 1929.

Typography and design by
Deb Figen, Art & Design Service
Seattle, Washington

Printing by Amica International

Printed in Korea